A 30-DAY DEVOTIONAL FOR SOPHOMORES

SOPHOMORE

STEPPING INTO MATURITY

LARS ROOD

simply for students

YouthMinistry.com/TOGETHER

Sophomore
Stepping Into Maturity

© 2013 Lars Rood

group.com
simplyyouthministry.com

Credits
Author: Lars Rood
Executive Developer: Nadim Najm
Chief Creative Officer: Joani Schultz
Editor: Rob Cunningham
Cover Art and Production: Veronica Preston

ISBN   978-0-7644-9003-3

10 9 8 7 6 5 4 3 2 1   20 19 18 17 16 15 14 13

Printed in the U.S.A.

TO ANNELIESE:

I'm scared to admit that when you get to this age, I'm going to want to hide you from people. You are already an amazingly beautiful and intelligent girl, and I'm pretty sure I will never be ready for you to be 16. Fortunately, I have a whole bunch of years to prepare for that time—and for the speech I'm going to be giving to boys who ask you out.

CONTENTS

INTRODUCTION

The sophomore year is so weird. You aren't a freshman anymore, which is great, but you don't really have any sort of distinct place in the school. You aren't an upper classman and you don't really want to be categorized with the freshmen, so you're kind of on your own. Some people would say that the 10th grade year feels like a holding pattern: You are just trying to get through it as best you can so you can rule the school the next two years. But you still have to figure out who you are going to be. In this devotional, we are going to focus on what it means to step into maturity, something specific to pursue this particular year.

A friend once told me that the sophomore year is so tough because it is the year you really choose if you want to grow up. You can either continue to act like a freshman and be lumped in with them, or start looking toward being more mature like juniors and seniors. For some students this is a pretty easy decision to make because they want to be seen as more mature, but for others this is a rough season to go through.

We all know one thing that happens during this year: You turn 16 (most of you will, anyway). That means you could get a driver's license. That is a major milestone in the life of most teens, and one of the reasons we are focusing on maturity.

I fully recognize that some of you are going to be frustrated when you read that the goal of this devotional year is for you to become more "mature." Yes, that seems to imply that I don't currently think you are mature. I know that may not be true for all of you. Some of you are relatively mature and have a lot of your faith journey and life journey figured out. If that's you, I'm stoked because you are starting with a leg up on everyone else. But if you are like I was my sophomore year, you probably have some good maturing to do.

How this book works:

This devotional includes 30 short things for you to think about. For each reading you'll find some sort of story and some follow-up questions to consider. You can do these by yourself, but you also can benefit from discussing them with a small group of people. This book might become 30 weeks of curriculum or simply provide 30 days of focus before the school year starts.

Each devotion includes a section called "The World Thinks." Most often these are comments that I have heard from non-Christians about these particular topics or issues. I don't hold back, so they may come across as a little negative. That's OK. You'll hear negative things all the time about your faith. The point is to encourage you to think through what people say and work out how you might respond to the thoughts and reactions people have about your faith in Christ.

You'll also find an action step for each devotion that is exactly what it sounds like: an opportunity to actually do something to discover and apply key truths. Often these are things that take some effort to accomplish and can help you grow. I want to encourage you to really put effort into doing them. Finally, I've included some Bible passages for you to look up—sometimes several, but usually just one or two. I want you to go deeper and explore other places in the Bible with more thoughts, stories, truths, and ideas that will help you.

It's my hope and prayer that these devotions will challenge you, encourage you, and put you in places where you will have the opportunity to mature in your faith.

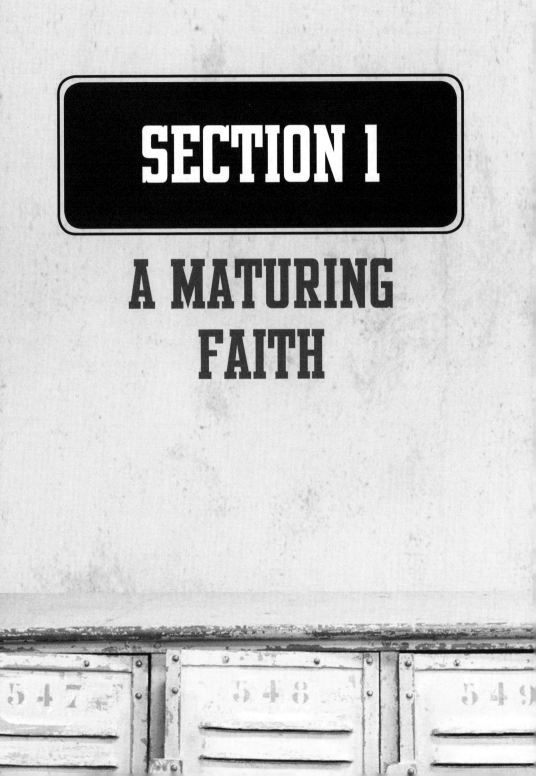

SECTION 1

A MATURING FAITH

What does a mature faith really look like? I'm going to go out on a limb and say that I don't really know. And that's not a cop-out on my part, because I am fully convinced that nothing is ever "mature," only "maturing." I can tell you what it looks like when you are growing in faith, so that's where I want to start. A maturing faith, in my opinion, is one that is moving toward Jesus. It's a faith that has legs and is going somewhere. You don't need to have everything figured out, but you do need to be growing. This probably means you are interested in how the Bible connects to your life as a sophomore. It means you are starting to care about your friends who don't know Jesus. It means you recognize that the place of meaning in your life is rooted in your faith in God, and you start to ask questions about how that applies to your future.

I can't offer you three steps that will mature your faith; I can only say that you will need to own your faith at some point and that your faith has to move beyond something you do just because that's what your parents do. During your sophomore year, a lot of faith-formation questions start to come around. You will, I hope, be around people who allow you to ask difficult questions. If you read the *Freshman* devotional that's part of this series, you know that I believe doubt is OK. You need the freedom to talk about what you believe and don't believe. That's how you mature.

№1 WHERE DO YOU LOOK FOR TRUTH?

If you're like me, you don't always know how to find out if things are true. Recently, though, I've noticed an interesting pattern happening with my own kids: When we are in the middle of a discussion on a road trip and someone makes a statement about a fact that sounds like it couldn't possibly be true, someone else in the car will instantly say, "Dad, Google® that and check it out." Because we live in a culture where smartphones are common, it's easy to look up "facts" about things, find out what's true or accurate, and then go on with the conversation.

But those aren't the only kinds of questions about truth that confront us, right? What if you are trying to figure out whether or not you're going to drink alcohol or follow a certain group of friends or place your own desires ahead of everyone else's needs? An online search engine isn't very helpful if you're doubting your faith, trying to figure out your role in the world, or trying to determine if some major decision is right for you. What matters is where *you* look for truth right now. I'm hoping that thinking this through will help you grow.

THINK ABOUT:

1. What is something you wish you knew the truth about?

2. What are some resources you use to try to find truth?

3. How do you think your parents figured out truth when they were your age?

THE WORLD THINKS:

Truth is up to you to decide. You can't look to anyone or anything to define it for you. What might be true for others doesn't necessarily have to be true for you. The only person who has the right to decide for you is you.

ACT:

Find an adult. It doesn't have to be a parent. It could be a coach, a boss, a youth leader, or a neighbor. Ask them this hard question: "When you were my age, how did you go about figuring out truth?" If you don't feel like you got a good answer from one person, go and ask another.

READ:

Psalm 25:5, Psalm 43:3, John 4:23, and Ephesians 6:14

№.2 WHAT PART OF YOUR FAITH IS EXCITING?

A few years ago on a mission trip to Mexico, my whole youth group bailed out on an evening meeting and drove to the beach to have tacos. Looking back I realize that both the drive to the beach and eating at a taco stand weren't probably the safest things we could have done that night, but it was a memory that all those students still talk about. We did it for one simple reason: I wanted to show them that being a Christian and serving God doesn't have to be boring and hard. The Christian life can have excitement. It's often when we lose any sort of that excitement that our faith becomes stale and boring.

Ask yourself this question: If your faith was 100 percent determined by how much you enjoyed getting up on Sunday mornings and going to church, would your faith be pretty boring? Mine sure would. There are times when the simple things of faith will have to sustain you—habits and disciplines such as reading your Bible, praying, meditating, and spending quiet time alone. But I believe that even those things can be very exciting. You may have an incredibly busy and full life, and thinking about that upcoming retreat with your youth group where you will have the opportunity to slow down and think—that's exciting to you. The goal is to think through where that excitement starts and make sure that you include it in your spiritual rhythm.

THINK ABOUT:

1. What specific things in your Christian life do you find the most boring and difficult to do? Why?

2. Are there ways that those things could become more exciting and give you more energy?

3. What specific parts of your faith are exciting and give you energy? Why?

THE WORLD THINKS:

Church can be really boring. Christians are mostly boring. The whole Bible is a book telling you what you can't do, and it puts so many restrictions on your life.

ACT:

As you responded or listened to others respond to question 3, I hope it sparked something in you with at least a little bit of excitement. The goal with this action step is two-fold. First, take that thing and do it. Simple enough, right? If you are in a youth group or attend a church, see if you can get someone to help make it a reality. Second, look at the things that you find boring and come up with one idea that could give it a little more life. It could be as easy as donuts before service on a Sunday morning or lunch after church. Take time to figure this one out.

READ:

1 Chronicles 29:22, Ezra 6:16, Psalm 16:11, and Ecclesiastes 11:9

№.3 WHO ARE YOUR MENTORS?

Paul taught me to love people. Evan taught me to love life. Tom taught me to work hard. Tony taught me to enjoy music. Eddie taught me to start over. Dan showed me how to slow down. Shane taught me to let others care for me. John taught me to think differently. Jack showed me that I had value. Marko helped me see my future. Roger gave me a chance. My dad showed me how to work hard. My mom showed me how to stand strong. I've learned a lot of things from a lot of people.

That list isn't even complete; I know if I'd taken more time to fill it out, I would have added in a lot of other people. The question for you to think about here is who is teaching you and what you are learning from them. You might be surprised at the things you learn from people that you never expected to teach you anything.

THINK ABOUT:

1. What people are you learning from now? What specific truths or lessons are you learning?

2. What does the word *mentor* mean to you? Why?

3. Is anyone learning from you? How are you helping that person (or those people) to grow?

4. Who in your life would you like to learn from? Why?

THE WORLD THINKS:

I'm tempted to say here that the world thinks you have to figure things out on your own. I believe that's an accurate statement, but I also think the world would say that you can learn from some people—but then would point you to people who may not be right for you or whose opinions run contrary to God's desires.

ACT:

Write down three things that you would like to learn. They might be new skills or characteristics, or they might be deficiencies you want to overcome. After creating that list, write a name next to each one and then go and ask that person to help you grow in that area.

READ:

Genesis 21:20, Exodus 17:12, and Hebrews 4:16

NO.4 WHAT ROLE DOES JESUS PLAY IN YOUR LIFE?

When I was a sophomore in high school, my youth group was a pretty big deal in my life. One morning after Sunday school, instead of going to the worship service as expected, we decided to hang out in the youth room and play bumper pool. About 10 minutes into the worship service, the choir director came storming into the room and yelled, "Is this a church or a pool hall?"—completely calling us out for skipping church and forcing us to make a quick decision about what was important. We all followed him to the service, and never again did we pull that stunt.

I tell that story to illustrate how I faced a defining moment that helped me decide I wasn't going to play around with this faith journey anymore. From that moment forward, I took my faith seriously for the rest of high school. You may be in a place right now where you go to church with your parents, or maybe the important part of church is your youth group and friends, like it was for me. That's an OK place to be, but ultimately you must answer the question of where Jesus fits in your life. How you answer that question has big ramifications for the way you live the rest of your life and the way you make decisions. I hope you don't end up getting shamed into making that decision like I was, but it worked for me and I'm still glad it happened.

THINK ABOUT:

1. If your life was a car and Jesus was in it, which seat would he be sitting in, and why?

2. What role do you see Jesus playing in the life of your parents and family?

3. Answer truthfully: Right now, how important do you think Jesus is going to be in your life after high school graduation?

THE WORLD THINKS:

Compartmentalize your life. Keep all the areas separated. Everyone does it. Make sure you have the right answers for Sunday school and youth group, but don't feel the pressure to be that Christian kid everywhere. You can choose to be who you want when you want, and Jesus doesn't have to play a big role in your life, anyway.

ACT:

Find a high school senior you respect, and ask that person what role Jesus has played in his or her decision on what to do after high school. You might find out that it's a big deal, but it might not be. Then ask an adult what role Jesus has in his or her big life decisions, and see what that person says.

READ:

Matthew 9:15, Matthew 14:27, Luke 12:22, and Galatians 2:16

NO.5 HOW COMFORTABLE ARE YOU WITH DOUBT IN YOUR FAITH?

I don't think I ever really doubted if God existed. But I do distinctly remember doubting if God actually cared about me. I was at a place of a lot of pain, and I felt like my world was starting to fall apart. My parents were going through a rough patch in their marriage, and I was asking questions about my future that I wasn't prepared to ask. During that season, I doubted if God really cared. Fortunately for me, I had a group of friends whose faith was stronger than mine—people who cared about me and built me up when I couldn't do it myself.

Doubt is an OK thing, so don't ever let anyone tell you that it's not. I'm convinced that God is OK with our doubts. Some amazing things have happened in my life when I was really wondering about things and God clearly showed up to open doors and meet my needs. Often in our doubts we can grow as we look to others or at least beyond ourselves for truth.

THINK ABOUT:

1. What are some doubts you have about faith, God, or Jesus right now? How long have you been wrestling with those doubts?

2. Where are some possible places you think you could find answers?

3. How do you think God, your parents, your friends, or leaders at your church feel about your doubts? Why?

4. How might those people in question 3 help you work through doubts and questions?

THE WORLD THINKS:

So much of life is a mystery that we can never unravel. You will never truly have any answers to your questions. If you think you will get answers, you are fooling yourself. Doubt is your mind's way of telling you that something is likely not true.

ACT:

Take a piece of paper and write down five doubts you have about your faith. (It's OK if you can't think of five doubts—this is still a worthwhile action step.) Then ask someone else to do the same thing. Compare your answers. See if you can have a discussion where you both talk about your doubts and help each other. If you have a youth worker or small group leader, ask them about their doubts, too.

READ:

Matthew 21:21, John 20:24-29, and Jude 1:22

NO.6 DO YOU HAVE A CHURCH OR FAITH COMMUNITY WHERE YOU ARE KNOWN?

One thing I know is that it is difficult to have a strong faith if we grow in it alone. We are called to be in community, and that's why the church isn't a building; it is a gathering of Christ-followers, people who are in this together. When I was in high school my youth group was a big part of my life. I can't remember ever missing a youth group night, event, camp, or trip. I went to everything, and I was truly known there. As I got older my youth group and church showed me a lot of talents and strengths that I hadn't recognized in myself yet. My church "knew" me in a way I didn't know myself and helped me to embrace part of me that I didn't even know existed. Being in a church or faith community where people know your name, welcome you, and walk alongside you through your journey is a big deal. Trying to do any journey alone is so much more difficult than being with others.

THINK ABOUT:

1. What adults at your church know your name?

2. How involved are you in a faith community, church, or youth group? How has your level of involvement increased or decreased in the past year?

3. What benefits do you see to being involved with others?

4. How can you get more engaged?

THE WORLD THINKS:

Be careful about getting involved with a church because they probably will tell you what you have to believe. And you don't want to get too close to others because they will let you down.

ACT:

The action step for this one is pretty simple. If you already are involved in a church, youth group, or faith community, look for others who are not and see if you can get them involved. If you are not involved, take a look at some options and see where you might want to get connected. It's important as you step into maturity.

READ:

Ecclesiastes 4:12 and Acts 2:41-47

⚊7 IN WHAT WAYS DOES YOUR FAITH GROW?

My faith grows at camp. It's always been that way for me. As a high school student, I was always looking with anticipation toward my youth group's next camp or retreat. During those weekends, the messages, music, and conversations helped me to grow closer to God. Even though I grew up in the church, it was on a camp weekend that I placed my faith and trust in Christ. As a youth pastor, camp continues to hold great meaning. I try to make sure that every quarter we have a camp/retreat type of experience for students where we show them Jesus and remind them about their faith.

But maybe that's not how it works for you. You may be someone who needs quiet times of reflection for reading, praying, or journaling. Or maybe you love to be outdoors and you see God's hand in the beauty of the world. Maybe it's a small group or a mentor/leader who shares their testimony, and that challenges you in a good way. There are many ways to grow in your faith, so strive to figure out which ideas and strategies work best for you—and also recognize when you are changing and need to try other things.

THINK ABOUT:

1. In what ways does your faith grow?

2. What things do you find don't help right now?

3. If you are feeling down in your faith, what can you do to jump-start it?

4. What people in your life know about the things that make your faith grow? How can those relationships help you grow?

THE WORLD THINKS:

Faith doesn't grow. You either have it or you don't. How do you decide what to put your faith in, anyway? Seems like it's a crapshoot.

ACT:

Find a youth leader or mentor this week, and ask him or her to help you come up with a list of new ways you could try to help your faith grow. He or she may have resources and ideas that you don't have and likely can point you in the direction of things you've never tried.

READ:

Matthew 6:25-34, Matthew 9:27-33, Luke 17:6, and John 14:12

№.8 WHERE DO YOU SERVE AND GIVE BACK?

Serving and giving back are essential choices in stepping into maturity and growing your faith. I remember a time in college when I helped out at a shelter one evening with a friend. We were working at a drop-in facility where people received referrals to places that had open beds. I'm not sure why, but that particular night things were really crazy on the streets; we had to deal with fights and a lot of major drama as we tried to serve and do our jobs. I remember at the end of the night driving home with my friend and asking, "What just happened?" The previous four hours had been like nothing I'd ever experienced. But even in that craziness, I knew we were exactly where we were supposed to be.

I've been on mission trips all over the United States and around the world, and I've taken students to so many different places. It's often on those trips that I see teenagers shine in ways I didn't expect. One year in Mexico I remember crossing the border with one particular student just wondering how he was going to be and secretly thinking this trip was going to be really tough on him. That student became the all-star of the trip, playing soccer and loving children nonstop for the whole week. You may already have ways that you give back, but if not, let me encourage you to serve—it is such a rewarding and growing experience.

THINK ABOUT:

1. Where have you served or given back in the last year?

2. How did you feel while serving or giving back?

3. What are service opportunities you know you enjoy doing, and why do you enjoy them?

4. How can you determine specific ways to serve and give back this week?

THE WORLD THINKS:

What do you have to offer? Why don't you let the professionals serve and you just go on being a little sophomore? You just want to serve because it makes you feel better, but the reality is that you don't make much of a difference.

ACT:

Lead the charge. How can you motivate the people around you or in your church or youth group to serve? Find an adult or other students that can help you, and figure out what you can do. Maybe you could partner with existing ministries at your church or in your community. Or maybe you could launch something new. Make phone calls, find the needs, and get serving. You have much to offer.

READ:

Joshua 24:14, Matthew 20:25-28, and John 12:26

№9 WHOM ARE YOU LEADING?

There is something about a mature faith that other people look at and want to have. They want to follow and experience that same kind of relationship with Jesus themselves. You might think that as a sophomore you don't really have much to offer to others and that no one wants to follow you. But that just isn't true. At my church we have a number of high school students who serve every week in our preschool Sunday program. They perform dramas, read Scripture, and do simple things such as sound effects for programs. When I watch them lead, I'm always inspired because it makes me think about my faith when I was their age—and they are way beyond where I was!

As you think about the people you are leading, expand what that even means. You may be on a sports team with teammates who are younger students. How are you leading them? You may be serving in your church and leading there. You could even be leading in your own home if you have younger brothers or sisters. How you interact with them is a form of leading, so lead well.

THINK ABOUT:

1. Where in your life do you have leadership roles?

2. How do you think others feel about your leading them?

3. In what areas would you like to take on more roles in leadership? Why?

4. Who are some leaders in your life that you look up to? Why do you admire them?

THE WORLD THINKS:

People follow strong leaders who have it all figured out. If you are not strong, loud, and focused, you can never be a leader. Just sit back, don't make waves, and get ready for a lifetime of following.

ACT:

It's time for some evaluation. Are you currently in any leadership roles? If not, what can you do to begin serving and how do you think your service can open the doors for leadership? If yes, what people are you leading and how can you begin releasing them to lead, too?

READ:

Exodus 13:17-18, Deuteronomy 3:28, Psalm 23:1-3, and Luke 11:2-4

№.10 WHAT IS YOUR NEXT BIG FAITH STEP?

This is the point of your story as a sophomore that you have to choose who you are going to be. A few years ago on a mission trip, I was in a room with a group of sophomore guys next to a room of freshman guys. As part of our evening devotionals, we encouraged our 10th-graders to begin thinking about how they would step into leadership and grow in the youth group. The only other option we told them was to simply revert back to being a freshman—and who would want to do that? Well, about three days into the seven-day trip, two of the guys from our cabin moved next door to be with the ninth-graders. They literally decided on that trip that they weren't ready to grow and didn't want to make any steps forward.

I hope that doesn't describe you. You are reading through these stories and devotions, and I trust that they are causing you to think about things and contemplate what a next step in your journey might be. I mentioned before that when I was a sophomore, my big faith step was never missing church. I decided it was going to be important to me, and it became a major step. Then I ultimately decided to go to a Christian college because that felt like the natural next step for me. I encourage you to consider what your next step might be—and then take it!

THINK ABOUT:

1. What are some next steps you might want or need to take?

2. Is anything in your life or faith holding you back from taking a next step?

3. How might you need support from others in order to take the next step?

4. What was your last step? Take a moment to celebrate that.

THE WORLD THINKS:

Just make sure that whatever steps you take in life ultimately help you succeed in what really matters: getting into college and landing the right job that pays lots of money. You will eventually walk away from your faith like most 20-year-olds do, so don't do anything that will hinder your future success.

ACT:

The thing about "steps" is that they require you to actually do something. Think through some big steps that will help your faith grow and help you step into maturity. Put together a little chart or write a few things on a piece of paper that you know would help. If you can't figure those out on your own (which is totally OK), ask someone else to help you think through it.

READ:

2 Chronicles 20:20, Matthew 6:30, Matthew 15:21-28, and Romans 1:17

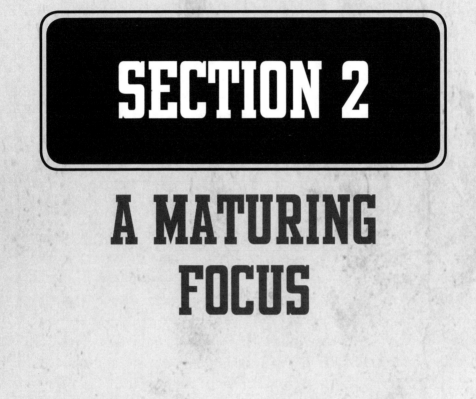

SECTION 2

A MATURING FOCUS

Probably the best way to describe this section is that it's about the season when your focus starts turning away from yourself and toward the rest of the world and other people. I remember when this started to happen for me. Up until this point, I was relatively self-centered and the world revolved around me, my wants, and my needs. But all of the sudden I had to start coming to grips with a world that didn't always care about me and who I was—a world that had a lot of pain and hurt and things I didn't understand. As I began to refocus myself and realized that there was actually a lot in my world that didn't always make sense, I started looking toward other people who could help me identify truth and experience a reality that did make sense.

So the maturing focus is about starting to turn outward and away from ourselves. Phrased another way, it's time to think about the things that Jesus cares about. Consider how you can make things better for other people and how your faith—which may still be simple—can make a difference. At your school, start genuinely caring about the people who are there and not just about the friends and small circle that you live in. Let your focus change, to start being aware of those who are clearly in need and don't seem to fit in. Attempt to look at things from other people's perspectives. Explore things that you don't understand or believe, and discover if you are OK with answers that don't always make sense.

№.11 WHO ARE YOUR ROLE MODELS?

I think it's interesting how we choose role models. Years ago I saw a video clip of an Olympic runner who was clearly hurt and coming into the stadium in last place. But she was determined to finish. When she entered the stadium for the last lap, everyone started clapping and cheering for her determination. I remember watching that and thinking I wanted to be like her. Though I'm not a runner like that, I saw in her this intense desire to finish what she started. She became a role model for me.

I also have a youth worker friend a few years older than me who has been doing youth ministry for almost twice as long as I have. Mike always surrounds himself with younger people and is the kind of person that I really desire to be like. He's selfless and giving and provides all kind of opportunities for people that they probably couldn't get on their own. He uses his longevity and resources to build others up. I love that.

I don't know who your role models are, but I'm sure you have some. Perhaps you have had a number of them through the years. That's pretty normal. Early on maybe it was a parent and then it switched to an athlete or someone famous for something else. The big questions you have to ask yourself: What key qualities does that person possess? And why are those qualities attractive to you?

THINK ABOUT:

1. Who are some role models you've had in your past? What did you learn from them?

2. Who are some of your role models today?

3. What qualities about them are important to you? Why?

4. How can you be a role model for others? What traits do you have that you think are worth following?

THE WORLD THINKS:

Follow celebrities. They have somehow figured it out, and since everyone's goal should be to become famous, learn from them and do what they do. But be your own person, too. Just pick and choose things you want to learn from others and blend them together. Be yourself—while imitating others.

ACT:

Ask some adults in your life who their role models were growing up. Ask them to explain why each person was significant to them. What did they learn from those role models? Then ask them what type of role model they feel they are for others. Spend some time with a piece of paper and write out some of your good traits and how you might be a role model for others.

READ:

Ezekiel 28:12, 1 Thessalonians 1:4-7, and 2 Thessalonians 3:9

№.12 HOW DO YOU SET HEALTHY PATTERNS?

Get up at 6 a.m. to read the Bible and pray. Fall asleep doing it at 6:05. Pray every night before going to bed. Fall asleep three minutes after starting. These were some of my patterns when I was in high school. I just wasn't very good at the things people said I needed to do in order to see my faith grow stronger. These patterns didn't work for me, and as much as I tried, I continued to fail.

I'm not sure about you, but I find it very difficult to do things early and late. I just can't seem to be focused either time. I hope that you know that is OK. It took me a while to figure that out for myself. I continued to struggle and feel bad about it, but finally one day I realized I had to set my own patterns and not just take ones that work for others. So I don't pray first thing in the morning. Yes, you read that correctly. I don't pray early in the morning. I find that my best time for focused prayer and reading my Bible is around 10 a.m. By that time I've woken up, eaten, had coffee, and gone through my morning emails at work. I can slow down and take time to focus then. That is a healthy pattern for me.

Same thing goes for working out for me. I don't like to do it in the morning or the evening. I find that about 4 p.m. every day is really my sweet spot for going to the gym. I generally need a change during that time and it's a good transition point between work and home life for me.

So the key is to know which patterns work for you and which don't. Don't feel guilty if you aren't a 6 a.m. prayer person or a 10 p.m. Bible-reading person. Discover what patterns work best for you, and then cultivate those habits that strengthen your faith and help you step into maturity.

THINK ABOUT:

1. What are some healthy patterns—spiritual, physical, social, or any other category—you have set?

2. How did those patterns get established, and how have they helped you?

3. What are some patterns you've tried that haven't worked?

4. What are some different possibilities you could try that might work for you?

THE WORLD THINKS:

Don't worry about patterns. Just do what works for you when it works for you, and stop it when it doesn't. You don't need to be concerned with doing anything in order to get better or grow or improve; it should just happen.

ACT:

For one week, pray and read your Bible at a different time each day. See if you feel best in the morning, mid-morning, lunch, afternoon, or after dinner. Discover what works for you. Maybe it'll change each week. Patterns can do that. But try a number of different things to see what works.

READ:

Exodus 25:40, Romans 12:1-2, Philippians 3:17, and 2 Timothy 1:13

№13 WHAT DO YOU THINK ABOUT DATING?

"Donna Loves Me." I no longer have the T-shirt that my sophomore-year girlfriend gave me, but I wish I did because it's such a good example of high school dating. Donna was my first girlfriend. She drove an orange Ford® Pinto and was a year older than me. She was in my youth group, and we dated for a couple of months. The summer we dated, I was playing in a big church softball league game, and right beforehand she gave me this orange shirt with black felt letters that said how she felt about me. I was obligated to wear it so I did—but only that one time. Then it went in a drawer—and we broke up.

Dating was a weird thing for me in high school. I didn't have a lot of girlfriends, but I did date and had a lot of my identity wrapped up in having a girlfriend. If I could define exactly what it meant for me, I would say that my overall thought about dating was "at least this girl likes me." It gave me some sort of self-worth that a girl noticed me and that I wasn't alone. Up until high school I'd always felt pretty alone, so I jumped into the dating world pretty fast—and that continued through college. I fully recognize now that I probably didn't set the healthiest pattern. I wish I could go back and change it—or at least ask advice from others about what they thought about me wearing my "Donna Loves Me" shirt.

You may not have a "Donna Loves Me" (or "Dan Loves Me") T-shirt, but I know you've thought about dating. Maybe it's already part of your life. Maybe it's just something you want. Maybe you're unsure if you're ready. It's something worth considering and discussing seriously, not jumping into just because "everyone else" is dating or because you feel a void that you want to fill.

THINK ABOUT:

1. How do you feel about dating as a sophomore?

2. Have you had a boyfriend/girlfriend, and if so, how long did the relationship last?

3. If you had to give one reason for dating, what would it be? If you had to give one reason against dating, what would it be?

4. How could you "date" and get to know others in safer ways than just having a boyfriend/girlfriend?

THE WORLD THINKS:

Date everyone you can and anyone you want. As a sophomore, you need to start worrying about your social standing in school, and getting invited or having a pool of people you can invite to dances is important. Make sure to "try out" a lot of relationships before you get married.

ACT:

If you are involved in a youth group or faith community, see if your leaders will set up a panel on dating where you can pose questions to some wise, Christ-honoring adults. Maybe even offer an anonymous box where you and your friends can drop your questions in advance and have the panelists answer them. Also, now might be a good time to start writing out a list of qualities you want in a future boyfriend/girlfriend. You might be amazed at how having that kind of list can help you make good choices.

READ:

John 15:13 and Hebrews 13:4

№14 WHAT ROLE DOES YOUR FAITH PLAY IN HOW YOU SEE THE WORLD?

I grew up on an island in Washington. We weren't completely isolated, but we didn't have cable TV or the Internet back then. (Yeah, I realize that's pretty much impossible for most of you to imagine.) In school we took a class on current events that required us to read Newsweek magazine every week. I remember thinking how much the events in the magazine didn't really impact my life at all. Everything felt so far away and unimportant to where I grew up.

My faith as a sophomore was quite similar. I had just decided to make my faith something real to me, but I didn't really know how it should or could impact the way I saw the world. I struggled, and no one spent much time helping me understand how the Bible connected to my life and the world I was growing up in. I just didn't understand how my faith in Jesus was relevant to the world.

Maybe you are in that same place—your faith and the world feel like they are islands apart. You might be like me, and you're having a hard time drawing connections between things. I hope this reading helps you think and talk about how these connections can happen. Don't give up! Jesus, Scripture, your faith—it all *does* relate to your world.

THINK ABOUT:

1. What is one specific way your faith influences how you see the world?

2. If you had to describe what it meant to see the world through the "lens" of Jesus, what would you say?

3. How well can you explain your faith—including how it leads you to make choices—to someone who is not a follower of Jesus?

THE WORLD THINKS:

There is no connection between what you do on Sunday mornings and the rest of the week. The church and your faith in Jesus don't really have anything to do with your real life. You can believe whatever you want, but when it really comes down to it, you just have to figure out how to live in this world independent of your beliefs.

ACT:

Find some older adults that you respect. It would be great if they run or own businesses, or have lots of responsibilities in their jobs or in their community involvement. Ask them how their faith impacts their work and their lives. Ask your parents and any other willing adults the same question. Hearing from multiple people is incredibly helpful in gaining wisdom and perspective in this area.

READ:

Psalm 24:1, Psalm 89:11, Jeremiah 10:12, and John 3:16

№.15 HOW ARE OTHER CHRISTIANS' STORIES HELPFUL TO YOUR FAITH?

I read a story years ago that really helped my faith grow. It was the biography of this guy named Keith Green, called *No Compromise*. Basically it told the story of how Green became a Christian in the 1970s and how he decided that if he was going to be a Christian, he wouldn't compromise anything for his faith. He ended up becoming an influential musician in the church, and a number of his songs are still sung today. His story impacted me because it was so powerful to read how he had changed from being a hippie to being a follower of Christ—and then ultimately dying at the age of 28 in a plane crash. I finished the book just thinking about how much more he could have accomplished if he hadn't died so young.

Stories of Christ-followers have always helped my faith mature. Just a couple of years ago I read *Blue Like Jazz* by Donald Miller, which is essentially his story as a young adult wrestling with what it meant to be a Christian. I was in a similar stage of life, and hearing about how he figured it all out was very helpful to my journey. As a student, you probably will have the opportunity to hear a lot of sermons and talks at church, camp, conferences, and retreats. Listen for the stories that are told. They can help you grow and mature.

THINK ABOUT:

1. How have you been impacted by the faith story of another Christ-follower? How did his or her story specifically impact you?

2. Why are stories so helpful in our growth as followers of Christ?

3. If you were asked to share a story right now about your own faith, what could you share that might help others to grow?

THE WORLD THINKS:

The world probably agrees that stories are helpful. Reality television is a great example of how we try to bring "real" stories to the world and learn from them. Unfortunately, so many of these shows are kind of fake and lack any serious meaning. Watch with a filter so you know what is and isn't real.

ACT:

Read and hear and pursue stories of other Christ-followers. For example, see if you can find the oldest person in your church, and ask them a list of questions about their faith journey as a teenager. They might have some amazing things to tell about the church or what it was like to be a Christ-follower when they were young. Think about what you can learn from their stories.

READ:

2 Peter 1:16-18

☰16 WHAT TAKES YOUR EYES AWAY FROM JESUS?

You probably have some things in your life that are really important and consume a lot of your time and energy. It might be a particular sport that you play well, and you've found yourself being added to more and more select teams. It could be that you have a boyfriend/girlfriend or just regular friends that you spend a ton of time connecting with. Maybe you are focused on school and that takes a lot of your time. These things aren't inherently bad, but they can take our focus away from Jesus.

My main challenge is simply being busy. I've always been a person who likes to do a lot of things, all the time. Through all of high school and beyond, I've continually bounced from one activity to the next without really ever having a lot of empty space to simply sit, relax, and think. Now that I'm a little bit older I have figured out how to create margin and space in my life, but back then it was so hard.

You may struggle with this, too. And when you add in homework, sports, practice, clubs, church, work, family, friends, social media, reading, and sleep—well, you just end up with a busy life, and any of those things can easily distract you from thinking about your faith or focusing on Jesus.

THINK ABOUT:

1. What things take the largest chunk of your time?

2. How much do you think about Jesus in the midst of your activities and busy life?

3. Do you have any specific ideas about how to create "balance" in your life and faith?

THE WORLD THINKS:

Fill your life with everything you can. You have to try everything to figure out what you are good at, what you do well. If you want to get into a top college or land a high-paying job, you are going to have to show them that you have diverse tastes and have been involved in many different things.

ACT:

I'm not telling you to quit things. In fact, I think it's a good idea to consider adding something else to your schedule—but it's probably not something you expect. I simply want you to add space for Jesus in the midst of your busy life. This may sound a bit cheesy, but it's important. Remember the Tim Tebow phenomenon where he dropped to his knee and prayed after scoring a touchdown? What if you simply thought more about Jesus in the midst of the things you were doing? You might find that some things suddenly would have less value to you. Or you may be attracted to try out something else. So this week come up with a plan for taking time for Jesus in the midst of being busy and doing things you like. You don't have to drop on the field and pray, but find what works for you.

READ:

Psalm 34:1-3 and Ecclesiastes 3:1-8

№17 HOW IMPORTANT IS JESUS TO YOUR FRIENDS?

My friends in high school all loved Jesus. That's what I always told myself because it took the pressure off me to have to choose new friends. There was some truth to that statement, though. Most of my friends went to youth group with me. We were a tightknit group, and at church we were pretty strong in our convictions. But most of those same friends were also the ones who were at all the parties with me.

I was a pretty good kid, but I still made a lot of bad choices with my "Christian" friends. The reality—as I saw it as a sophomore—was that we were all in the same boat trying to figure out how much youth group and church impacted our regular lives and if Jesus really had much role in our day-to-day experiences. Unfortunately, I discovered that a number of my friends who were really important to me didn't have a real connection to Jesus at all. Those were the friends that tended to get me in trouble the most. I did some dumb things for the sake of those friendships. Sadly, it was pretty easy for my friends to get me to go along with them; I was the kind of kid who really felt like he needed his friends because there just weren't a lot of other options.

Maybe your friends are helping you travel in the right direction, toward a mature faith in Christ. Maybe they're leading you in the wrong direction. Maybe it's somewhere in between. Take some time to ask yourself hard questions about how your friends are helping you or hurting you.

THINK ABOUT:

1. How important is Jesus to your closest friends?

2. If the answer is "not very," how does that impact you? If the answer is "a lot," how does that impact you?

3. Do you have any friends you believe you should walk away from? Why or why not?

4. What might be the potential long-term impact of having close friends whose beliefs are different from you?

THE WORLD THINKS:

Your faith is your faith, just like my faith—or my lack of faith— is my own. It really doesn't matter who you spend time with, so spend time with people from all kinds of faith backgrounds.

ACT:

I'm not asking you to judge your friends with this, but I would like you to put together a list of your closest friends and simply write next to their name if you think they follow Jesus or not. Then, in another column, write if you think that friend has a positive or negative impact upon you. Finally, write three things you can pray about for that friend.

READ:

Job 16:20, Psalm 41:9, Ecclesiastes 4:10, and 1 Corinthians 12:2

№.18 WHAT FUTURE CAREER WOULD YOU CHOOSE RIGHT NOW?

The other day I was sitting in my house, about two blocks away from Microsoft®, and I thought about my high school plans for my life. I loved computers and entered college as a computer science major, and if I had stayed on that track, when I graduated I could have started working at Microsoft before the company was worth so much. I probably would have received a lot of stock options and today might be a very wealthy person. Unfortunately, I'd probably be wealthy and miserable because working with computers is clearly *not* what God gifted me in or called me to do! But I don't think there was anything wrong with me choosing that career path in high school because when I got to college, God used a series of events to show me that working with students—first as a counselor, then a teacher, and finally as a youth pastor—was the direction he wanted me to go.

So go ahead. Take a moment and dream about your future. Then choose exactly what you think you should be doing. But hold it loosely. The future is God's and everything in it. To some of you that might be frustrating, but to others that brings a great hope. You don't have to have it all figured out now; you can dream and pray and ask God to provide you with his plans.

THINK ABOUT:

1. If right now you had to choose a career path for your future, what would you pick? Why?

2. What things would need to happen for you to make that future a reality?

3. If money, fame, power, and stability weren't deciding factors and you could choose one career or lifelong way to serve God, what would you pick? Why?

THE WORLD THINKS:

"You can do anything you want." We all hear this as early as we can remember. The world says it, but it's not true. For example, I couldn't be a rocket scientist because I'm simply not smart enough. I also couldn't be a ballet dancer because I don't have the skills it would take. The world wants you to believe that you can do anything, though, and that when you fail, it's your fault—it's not because of the way God created you to do other things.

ACT:

Find three adults and ask about their plans and dreams for the future when they were in high school. See if those plans lined up with what they actually have ended up doing. Discover how they feel about that.

READ:

Proverbs 24:14, Ecclesiastes 8:7, and Romans 8:38-39

NO.19 HOW CAN YOU STAY CONSISTENT?

If you did the *Freshman* book in this series, you might have noticed that some of these themes are repeated because they're important. That includes the topic of consistency, which is so significant in our faith journey. The sad reality is that many of us just don't know how to stay consistent. That's one of the reasons some people wonder why anyone even bothers with New Year's resolutions. We make the major decisions and statements about how we want to live our lives differently in the new year, yet within only a few weeks or months we often return to our old patterns of behavior. The changes we wanted to make just didn't last like we had wanted them to. Many people say that it takes about two months for something to change and become a pattern in our lives. As I write this, my gym is doing a two-month program on healthy eating and working out regularly to start this new year. Because I haven't been consistent on my own, I'm joining in, hoping that the community of people in my gym can help me make good choices.

But it is incredibly hard to change patterns. One thing I've learned over the years is that the best way to make it work is if you can come up with a real plan, let others know about it, and stick with it no matter what gets in the way. For you, a real plan might be to simply make the commitment that you will always go to youth group on Wednesday nights. Yes, things will get in the way. You will have too much homework, be studying for a test, or be really tired. You will have friends facing crises, your room will need to be cleaned, or you'll have a major breakout on your face. But consistency says that none of those things can get in the way of following your plan.

THINK ABOUT:

1. What are two specific things you want to stay consistent with?

2. What challenges typically hinder your consistency in those areas?

3. How can you stop things from getting in the way?

THE WORLD THINKS:

Do what feels right when it feels right, and don't feel any pressure to follow any pattern. You choose for yourself what works, and don't let anyone tell you there is anything you have to do.

ACT:

What is one thing you want to be consistent about this week or month? Write it down. What gets in the way for you? Write it down. How can you stop those things getting in the way? Write it down. Make five copies of that piece of paper. Hand them to five people you trust, and ask them to help you pursue consistency.

READ:

Philippians 3:17 and Hebrews 5:14

⒩⒪20 HOW DO YOU REFOCUS WHEN YOU HAVE STUMBLED OR STRUGGLED?

As a youth pastor it's often easy to see when students in the youth ministry are struggling with something. More often than not, they want to avoid me. They share less and generally have some sort of dark disposition about them. I can just tell with some sort of sixth sense that there is some struggle going on in their life and they are hurting. One of the toughest things as a youth pastor is when a student who has been so active and involved and whose faith looks like it's exciting and growing suddenly disappears. Unfortunately, over the years I've seen this happen so much.

The sad reality is that the last place a lot of us want to go when we are struggling is church because that's where we feel the most judged. What a wacky thing! At church we should feel the most loved, cared for, and surrounded by grace. But it often doesn't happen, causing us to feel out of place, judged, and falsely believing that God doesn't want us there around all the "good" people. Refocusing our faith can be hard because we sometimes get so far down a bad path that it's hard to get back. But with God nothing is impossible.

THINK ABOUT:

1. Have you ever felt like you shouldn't be going to church? Why or why not?

2. How have you refocused your faith when you have struggled?

3. What are some other ways you could refocus if you needed it?

THE WORLD THINKS:

Failure is not something Christians believe in. Most churches will tell you what they are against and not what they are for. They don't want you there if you mess up. Parents send their kids to church to be around "good" kids, and if you are always making mistakes, you are not one of them and you won't be welcome.

ACT:

It's good to learn and practice discernment. Do some friends or youth group members seem to be uncomfortable being at church? Do you know if they are struggling with something? How can you be welcoming and help provide a gospel of grace to them this week?

READ:

John 4:4-30

SECTION 3

MATURING DECISIONS

We all want people to trust us. I remember all the times in high school when I argued with my parents about trust. I felt like I deserved it; they wanted me to earn it. In this section we will consider how your faith can impact your decisions and help you as you are maturing. Please hear me when I say that you are only "stepping" here. You don't need to have this all figured out. Adults need to acknowledge that sometimes a few steps forward are accompanied by a couple of steps back. The goal is for you to be in situations where you are given the opportunity to start maturing in how you make decisions.

I want you to know that many adults fully recognize that we need to give you greater opportunities to shine and to make great decisions. We are sorry for what we've done to shrink your world and capabilities. You are much more credible, reliable, trustworthy, and solid than we sometimes admit. Take advantage of this stage of your life and show the world that you have the ability to do great things. Use these next 10 devotions alone or with a group to help mature the way you make decisions. Most of the action steps in this section will help you to show others that you are growing in this area.

NO. 21 HOW MUCH DO YOU THINK ABOUT YOUR DECISIONS?

Epic story for you: One Friday afternoon in college, I drove to my friends' house. When I got there, they asked me what I was doing for the weekend, and I told them that I was going home to see my parents. My friends said they had a proposal for me. If I would leave right then and drive them to San Francisco, they would pay for everything all weekend long. But the catch was I had to decide right at that moment because we needed to get on the road. Without even thinking about it I simply said yes, and we got in the car to start the 14-hour drive.

Don't you think that might have been a really good time to ask a couple of questions? The simplest one—"Why are we going to San Francisco?"—would have been a good place to start! But I didn't ask any questions and just trusted my friends that we were going for good reasons. Unfortunately, they had bad plans that I didn't find out about until halfway through our drive, and at that point I was committed to being their driver.

You may have gotten yourself into risky situations like this because you didn't think about something before you jumped in. But maybe you are the opposite: You *really* think through things and diagram all the possible outcomes of each and every decision. I've done that, too, with the potential good listed on one side of a paper and the bad on the other. Somewhere in between both of those extremes is where we make most of our decisions.

THINK ABOUT:

1. What's one decision that you wish you had taken more time to think about before making? What were the outcomes?

2. What decision did you have the most difficult time making? How did you end up making it?

3. Where does your faith fit into your decision-making process?

THE WORLD THINKS:

Don't think; just do. The people who are most successful in life don't spend a lot of time thinking about decisions; they just work hard at adapting to situations that they encounter. And even if you don't make the best choice every time, it's no big deal—you can live with the consequences.

ACT:

Ask someone older than you how they make decisions. See if they will discuss a decision they made that they regret and the reason they believe they made the wrong decision. Think about some decisions you are facing, and ask that person for advice on how to make the right call.

READ:

1 Kings 22:5, Psalm 16:7, Isaiah 16:3, and John 8:16

№.22 WHAT MISTAKES HAVE YOU LEARNED FROM MOST?

In the last reading, I told you about my decision to go to San Francisco without really thinking about it. It turned out that my friends admitted along the way that they were planning on buying some illegal things—and then I would have to drive them the 14 hours back home. I felt like I was committed to the trip and couldn't change my mind and turn around because they were my friends, but I was frustrated and angry the whole time because I believed they had lied to me. But it also was my own fault for not asking any questions.

Nothing major happened on the drive home, but I learned from that point forward to ask my friends a lot more questions when they attempted to get me to do something with them. I could have faced some negative consequences from my lack of asking questions and making a decision for myself. It was a huge mistake to go along with them, yet I did it anyway.

Mistakes don't always have to be major or illegal. I talked to a student once who simply told me that it was a mistake to have skipped winter camp that year. He told me that his faith was struggling a bit and the encouragement that comes from being at camp could really have helped him. He said he planned on not missing another camp. I'm not sure what kind of mistakes you've made, but the biggest issue in a life of maturing decisions isn't the mistake but what you learn from it. So, what are you learning?

THINK ABOUT:

1. What are some things you've learned from mistakes?

2. How is your learning helping to mature your decision-making processes?

3. Is there anything specific that you believe you've learned that could help others as they make decisions?

THE WORLD THINKS:

Everyone makes mistakes. Don't worry about it. Just roll with it and move on. There will always be more mistakes, and you will need to simply forget about them.

ACT:

Part of learning to make mature decisions is to show people that you can learn from your mistakes. Take one of the questions above and write a longer response. Then talk it over with a parent. You want your parents to trust you more? Show them what you are learning.

READ:

2 Samuel 11:1–12:13

№.23 HOW DO YOU MAKE TOUGH DECISIONS?

The toughest decision I've ever had to make in my life was to walk away from a serious relationship. I was engaged but knew that it wasn't right—I needed to break it off. But it was really difficult. As I look back I know I didn't really have the best process for making that decision. I didn't involve my friends, a pastor, my parents, or anyone else. That's probably why it was so hard—I didn't have anyone in my life who was confirming the decision for me.

That situation taught me that it is always better to involve other people in tough decisions, because on my own it is really difficult. I questioned my maturity and my issues. I really struggled, wondering if it was the right thing. After I had made the decision, though, my friends suddenly felt comfortable sharing with me their opinion and they all agreed I was right. But it would have been so much more helpful if I'd sought their feedback before I made that decision.

You may have a good process for making decisions already. You might have trusted friends, parents you can talk to, a youth leader who knows you well, a journal for processing your thoughts, or a solid connection to God. You may be mature for your age and have a good sense of discernment. I didn't. Whatever your level of maturity, think through how you make tough decisions and how you can mature in that area.

THINK ABOUT:

1. What's the toughest decision you've ever made? What made it so difficult, and how did you make your decision?

2. If you're facing a situation where you've been struggling to make a decision or find a solution, how can you involve some other people in the process?

3. How can you mature in your decision-making process— particularly when it comes to tough, difficult decisions?

THE WORLD THINKS:

Everyone gives advice. You have to choose what's right for you and not for others. If you can't make a decision, just use a search engine to do some research, because your story is probably not too different from others. See what they did, and then copy them.

ACT:

Go talk to your pastor. Ask them about the toughest decision they ever made and why it was so hard. Then ask them how they made it, and ask for prayer in the difficult situations you face.

READ:

Psalm 51 — this was written after David committed adultery with Bathsheba and arranged the murder of her husband

NO. 24 HOW DO YOU RESPOND TO CONFLICT?

I bottle things up and hide. That's always been the way I've done it. When I was a sophomore, I spent a lot of time in my room reading. I lost myself in books and just tried to avoid conflict at all costs. It was easy to simply go downstairs to my room after school, come up for dinner, and then go back downstairs. It's much harder for your generation because a lot of conflict follows you wherever you go. Text messages, social media, cell phone calls—they all bring it to you and make it harder to avoid. I could shut it out, but you live in a world where that is increasingly more difficult.

Over the years I've gotten better at dealing with conflict, but I'm still not perfect. I stew over things in my head for way too long. They get me riled up, and I often make the conflict worse because I became more frustrated in my head before going to someone and talking about it. Just recently I had to apologize to someone for something I had said, and I decided to call that person right away and say I was sorry. After the call, though, I realized that I hadn't done a very good job and had to call again to make sure the person clearly and accurately understood me.

We can't completely avoid conflict in life; it's going to happen. I'm not sure how you deal with conflict, but I hope you are able to bring things we learn from Jesus into it such as grace, mercy, love, and kindness. Those things all help.

THINK ABOUT:

1. What is the typical way you respond to conflict? How has your typical response changed in the past year or two?

2. As followers of Christ, we are called to live differently. What are some characteristics we are called to display that can help in conflict situations?

3. What is a conflict you are dealing with right now? How do you need to respond?

THE WORLD THINKS:

Conflict is a part of life. You don't have to get along with all people. If they can't handle you or the way you think, just walk away from them. It's their problem, not yours.

ACT:

Find a close friend and request a "conflict assessment." Ask your friend how he or she sees you deal with conflict, and ask for some tips and advice to do it better.

READ:

2 Corinthians 12:8-10 and Galatians 5:17

ℼ25 WHAT ROLE DO YOUR PARENTS PLAY IN YOUR DECISIONS?

I always had a good relationship with my parents in high school. They would tell me what to do, and I would do it. No problems, right? Truthfully, though, that was our process. I didn't make a lot of decisions; they made them for me. I look back now and realize that wasn't always the healthiest process, but it did work for us then. They trusted me because I was a pretty good kid who didn't get into a lot of trouble.

Unfortunately, this decision-making strategy didn't help me down the road. I reached a point in life where my parents weren't able to make decisions for me anymore, but I didn't have the skill set to make wise choices. I'd never learned to ask for help, and because of that I started this long journey of keeping everything inside.

You may be in a different place with your parents and feel like you can ask their advice and seek out their wisdom. That is a great place to be. You show them that you are willing to listen and learn when you go to them and ask for advice and help. That shows a maturity that likely will be rewarded in trust.

THINK ABOUT:

1. What's the last decision you made where you felt like help from your parents was very important?

2. How well do your parents know you and what you care about?

3. If you had a tough decision to make, how could you approach your parents for help?

4. If you don't have a good relationship with your parents, what other adult could you go to for help?

THE WORLD THINKS:

Times have changed. Your parents didn't grow up in the world you are living in, so they can't possibly understand the decision-making process you have to go through. Life is harder now; how could they possibly help?

ACT:

Come up with a list of three things you are trying to decide. They can be simple things or more difficult issues. Make sure at least one of them is a significant decision, such as what you will do after high school. Sit down with your parents (or another trusted adult, if you don't have a good enough relationship with your parents) and ask for help with the decisions. If you want to be seen as mature and want to grow in how you make your decisions, this will go a long way to demonstrate that you are maturing.

READ:

Proverbs 17:6, Ephesians 6:1-4, and 2 Timothy 3:2

NO. 26 ARE YOU A LEADER OR A FOLLOWER?

As you continue in this journey of learning to make more mature decisions, you'll eventually need to decide if you lead or follow. This decision is so important because it is hard to make good decisions all the time if you are simply a follower. As I shared earlier, I didn't always make great choices. That road trip to San Francisco was a low moment of me simply going along with what other people were planning. I was a follower and I potentially could have followed them into getting in a lot of trouble.

But it's true you also can get in trouble as a leader, right? I've done my fair share of leading my friends astray. We used to do some pretty dumb stuff in college that involved climbing things we shouldn't have climbed. I led quite a few people on some bad paths but was fortunate that no one got hurt. As a youth pastor and someone who has been a Christian for a long time, I have often seen students struggle with this issue of being a leader or a follower. Sometimes they don't understand the consequences of blindly following other people, but more often than not it seems they just haven't really ever been given any opportunities to serve in leadership type roles.

If you've never had the opportunity to lead chances, you may not know how to do it—or how to do it well. As I shared earlier, when my parents were making all the decisions for me, life was easier. When I had to start making major choices on my own, it was tough because I didn't know how to do it. Look for opportunities to lead, and go from being just a follower to being a leader.

THINK ABOUT:

1. What's an area in which you feel you've simply followed other people? Why haven't you led in that area?

2. Is there a group or an area in which you are a leader? How do you lead?

3. What are the benefits of being a follower? of being a leader?

4. In your maturing process, how might you need to grow as a leader?

THE WORLD THINKS:

Everyone wants to be a leader, but there just isn't enough space for that to happen. Some of you have to be followers. Deal with it.

ACT:

If you are in a youth group or small group, talk to your leader and ask if he or she can help you grow in the area of leadership. Maybe there is an upcoming camp, retreat, mission project, or event, and your leader can give you a role in leading something. Ask for advice and tips on how to lead. We all need help knowing how to lead well, and we all need to be taught.

READ:

Exodus 15:22, Numbers 14:8, and Joshua 1:6-9

№.27 WHO DO PEOPLE SAY THAT YOU ARE?

The other day I was looking at a bookmark that I've been using for a long time. It's from a summer camp I worked at, and all the staff wrote on it positive characteristics they saw in me. It's something that has always made me feel good about myself because they listed traits such as well-liked, courageous, friendly, and strong—characteristics that I am glad people see in me. Over the years this bookmark has sat on my desk, and when I'm feeling low or discouraged I pick it up and read through the list. At times I've read the things that were said about me and thought that I wasn't sure if they were still true. I guess I sort of use it as a barometer for working on those things a bit more.

I think all of us want to know that people have positive, good, encouraging things to say about us. We want to be liked, believed in, and trusted. When God created us, he created us in his image and called us good—and even though humanity's perfection was damaged by sin, God's design and his declaration form a great foundation to start from. Often what people say reflects what God did when he created us, but sometimes their words don't line up with how God sees us and we simply have to rely on and trust the things God says.

THINK ABOUT:

1. Who do people say that you are?

2. What are some things you wish people knew about you? Why are those things so important or meaningful to you?

3. What do you believe God thinks about you?

THE WORLD THINKS:

You define who you are, and you don't need to worry about what others think. Have thick skin because more often than not, others will try to bring you down to build themselves up.

ACT:

Talk with a few people in your life about how they perceive you in three categories. Ask them to be honest in what they think of you (1) as a person, (2) as a Christian, and (3) as a friend. What things do they say that you connect with, and what things are hard to hear?

READ:

Psalm 139

^{NO.}28 WHAT DECISIONS HAVE YOU MADE THAT YOU KNEW WERE RIGHT?

You may not get a lot of credit for decisions you are making as a sophomore, even when you make the right choices. Maybe you feel like nobody notices when you do something right and you only get feedback when you do something wrong. I can relate to that. In high school I was pretty quiet and was always just behind the scenes. I made what I think were a lot of good decisions my sophomore year to not get caught up in the party scene, to honor my parents and their decisions, to make good choices when it came to my girlfriend, and to be wise with resources and money.

I remember one time being with a group of my friends somewhere, and they were on the cusp of getting into trouble doing something I didn't think was right—so I just left and went home. I don't think I ever told my parents about the situation or talked to anyone about the good decision I made. It probably would have helped me earn some trust if my parents had seen that I had made a wise decision. Consider things that you've done right, and even though I'm not there in person with you, I definitely want to give you some credit and praise for those choices!

THINK ABOUT:

1. Think of something specific that you believe you did right. Why did you make that decision?

2. Do you believe you have received credit for the good decisions you've made? Why or why not?

3. Without always simply telling people about the good decisions you are making, how can you let other people—such as your parents—know so they can trust you more?

THE WORLD THINKS:

Whenever possible, take credit for the good things you do. Tell everyone when you do something right because you are likely going to fail again soon and you'll need to have something to balance your failures against.

ACT:

This might push you beyond your comfort zone, but I want you to write out two specific things you believe you did right. Give the reasons why you made those decisions, and then go and talk to your parents. If it feels weird, simply tell them that the writer of this devotional encouraged you to talk to them. Just tell them what you believe you did right, why you made the decision, and ask them how they feel about it. You will be amazed at how this proactive step can show your parents that you are maturing.

READ:

Psalm 5:12, Psalm 11:7, and Hosea 14:9

NO.29 DO YOU MAKE YOUR FRIENDS BETTER?

One mark of growing in maturity is making the people around you better—focusing less on yourself and more on those you care about and spend time with. I think of this as being similar to a point guard on a basketball team. That position's job is to set up other teammates to score by getting them the ball at critical moments when they can be successful. How good are you at making people around you better?

I have a few gifts that I think God has blessed me with that really help other people. One thing that I know God has called me to do is to be a "connector." That means I'm always thinking about people that should meet because they will benefit each other. So with my friends I often think about what connections I can make that will help them. I was this way in high school, too. I often spent time just wanting to provide the right resources or things for my friends. I hope this was seen as my way of caring for them. I wasn't perfect at it, but it is something that I started doing when I was pretty young. Take time to consider how you make people better—or how you can, if it's not something you're already doing.

THINK ABOUT:

1. What are some ways you make or can make your friends better? Give specific examples.

2. Are there specific gifts and talents God has given you that you believe can be used to better your friends? How are you using these gifts and talents—or how can you use them?

3. What is the benefit to you when you make others better?

THE WORLD THINKS:

This is a rough world, so it's OK to be a little selfish. Focus on yourself. You need to just worry about you and not about other people. Making it in this world will be all about you relying on yourself.

ACT:

On a piece of paper, write the names of two friends. What specific things could you do this week that would make them and their lives better? Without telling them what you are doing or why you're doing it, try it out and see what happens.

READ:

Job 16:20, Job 19:21, and Proverbs 17:17

№30 HOW MUCH DO PEOPLE TRUST YOUR DECISIONS?

This is the pinnacle, right? Wanting to be someone that others trust. We all want to know that people trust us when we make decisions. Even as a sophomore, you will be making decisions that you want people to believe in. Probably more often than not, you are looking for your parents to trust you. You want them to see that you are making mature decisions and growing in your faith. Although you might not be making huge, life-altering decisions this year, you still have to make choices about things—and the more consistently you make good ones, the more you will be trusted.

As I shared before, I didn't make a lot of major decisions in high school because my parents made most of them for me. This really hurt me as I got older because I didn't trust my own big decisions—I had no practice in making them. It was hard for me to trust myself because I'd never experienced doing anything through which I "earned" trust.

But once you start making decisions and discovering that you can do it well, it does feel good. You've made a decision that you feel is right. Maybe you asked people advice, got some different ideas, and ultimately got feedback from others that you did the right thing. Feels good—and gives you motivation and momentum to keep making good choices and continue stepping into maturity.

THINK ABOUT:

1. Why do people trust your decisions—or do they?

2. How have you grown as a result of thinking about maturing?

3. What is your next step in decisions you need to make?

4. How can you pursue consistency in making good decisions?

THE WORLD THINKS:

People will only trust you if you keep making the right decisions. As soon as you make one wrong one you will be back at the bottom on the trust ladder. Don't mess this up. You have a lot of pressure and consequences riding on this.

ACT:

Trust is one of those scary things: We all want it, but it is something that's often earned and not just given. So as a sophomore who's growing in your faith, focus, and decision-making skills, begin to verbalize those decisions with people around you. So go to a parent or another adult and ask them to rate you on your maturity level with your faith, focus, and decisions. Ask them to rate you on a 1-10 scale and then to give you advice.

READ:

Psalm 22:4, Psalm 40:4, Luke 16:10, and 1 Peter 2:6

FOLLOW-UP

Congrats! You've made it through a series of 30 devotions that I hope have challenged you to think about how you can "step into maturity" as a sophomore. These are simply some steps for you and not the final process that will get you there. But if you read through everything, answered the questions, tried out the action steps, and read the Scripture passages, I believe you're on the path to growth and maturity.

The sophomore year can be such a tough time. You may face setbacks and issues, but don't be discouraged or lose hope. You've got a long way to go and a long time to get there. My hope is simply that you are maturing in your faith, focus, and decisions. I'm praying for you.